FAITH RULES!

Faith in Action

Discovering Real-Life Heroes

by Judy Reed

In Celebration®

Author: Judy Reed
Editors: Angella Phebus, Alyson Kieda
Interior Design and Illustration: Robin Gale Wynsma
Cover Illustration: Daniel Vasconcellos

Send all inquiries to:
Children's Publishing
3195 Wilson Drive NW
Grand Rapids, Michigan 49544

Faith in Action: Discovering Real-Life Heroes
ISBN: 0-7424-2828-1

1 2 3 4 5 6 7 8 9 PHXBK 09 08 07 06 05 04

TABLE OF CONTENTS

INTRODUCTION

"What good is it, my brothers, if a man claims to have faith but has no deeds? Can such faith save him? Suppose a brother or sister is without clothes and daily food. If one of you says to him, 'Go, I wish you well; keep warm and well fed,' but does nothing about his physical needs, what good is it?…Show me your faith without deeds, and I will show you my faith by what I do"

(James 2:14–18).

All of us long for people to look up to, for heroes. Often, the people we choose to look up to are those we hear about on television or read about in the newspapers. Athletes, musicians, and Hollywood celebrities often fill the role of hero. Unfortunately, many of these celebrities are not good role models. They may be talented on the playing field, on the radio, or on the big screen, but they are missing something that no hero should live without—Jesus Christ.

In the pages that follow, you will find the stories of seven heroes of the faith. They are not heroes because of their talents or great deeds. They are heroes because they showed their faith through how they lived their lives.

So what traits does a hero of the faith have? The answer is many! Heroic traits include courage, determination, strength, dedication, loyalty, bravery, willingness to sacrifice, a wish to glorify Jesus, and love for humanity. Read the following stories closely and see if you can pick up what heroic traits each person possesses, and how each man or woman lived out their faith day by day.

The Secret Room
The Story of Corrie ten Boom

Heroic Quality: courage

"So do not fear, for I am with you; do not be dismayed, for I am your God. I will strengthen you and help you; I will uphold you with my righteous right hand" (Isaiah 41:10).

"Faith is like a radar the human eye cannot see."
—Corrie ten Boom

"Stop! Stop!" pleaded a voice. An explosion of breaking glass crashed loudly across the street.

Corrie ten Boom peeked out her window at a horrifying scene. The windows of Mr. Weil's fur shop were shattered across the sidewalk. As Corrie watched, German soldiers threw Mr. Weil's clothes in the street and loaded their arms with his furs! Corrie's heart sank. Mr. Weil was a Jew. The German Nazis hated the Jews and forced many of them from their homes and shops. Corrie knew she had to act quickly to get Mr. Weil away from the Germans to keep him safe. As soon as the Nazis left, Corrie hurried across the street and brought Mr. Weil back to her family's home above her father's watchmaker shop. Later, Corrie's brother sneaked him out of Germany by night.

This was just the beginning of Corrie and her family's efforts to help the Jews during World War II, when Adolf Hitler, the dictator of Germany, killed over six million Jews.

Hitler...had over six million Jews killed.

8

After Mr. Weil escaped with the help of Corrie's brother, more Jews found their way to the ten Boom home. Corrie loved God and his people. She was born in Holland in 1892, the youngest child of Casper and Cornelia ten Boom. She had two older sisters, Betsie and Nollie, and an older brother, Willem.

The ten Booms built a secret room in their home where Jews could hide from the German police. Corrie had to be very careful. The Germans were always watching.

Their constant scrutiny affected Corrie's work for God. Before the Germans first began monitoring citizens' actions, Corrie had been running several clubs for girls aged twelve to eighteen. The girls participated in gymnastics, music, walking, camping, and other activities. Corrie also shared God's love with them and encouraged them to go to God in prayer. When the Germans invaded Holland in 1940, Corrie was forced to close the clubs.

Then one day in 1944, the police came to search the house. The Jews staying there quickly hid. When the police did not find the Jews, they questioned Corrie. Though Corrie was beaten, she did not give the police the information they wanted.

Instead, she prayed, "Lord, Jesus help me."

"If you use that name again, I'll kill you," one of the men warned. But he stopped beating her. When the secret room could not be found, the police arrested the whole family and others from the town.

Most of the prisoners were later released. But Corrie and her sister Betsie were not. When Corrie appeared before a German officer, she prayed that God would show her what to say. She told the officer about her work with the girls' clubs and about God. The officer was curious and asked lots of questions. Corrie told him about Jesus and about forgiveness. After that, the man helped her but was not able to release her.

Corrie and Betsie were sent to a concentration camp called Ravensbruck. They were escorted into the prison, and miraculously Corrie made it past the guards with a small Bible. Corrie and Betsie were packed into a cold barracks room with 1,400 other women. The room was horrible to live in. It was originally built to hold only 400 people. The 1,400 women were forced to live in the small space crammed together. The straw mattresses were covered in thick dust, and they swarmed with fleas. The women were constantly being bitten.

Instead, she prayed, "Lord, Jesus, help me." "If you use that name again, I'll kill you," a policeman said.

The fleas were so bad that the guards kept out of the room. Because of this, the fleas became a blessing. Corrie was able to read the Bible to the other prisoners without worrying about the guards catching her.

The women in the camp worked very hard. Their long day began at 4:30 a.m. with roll call. If a woman failed to stand up straight, she was beaten with whips. During the day, the women loaded and unloaded heavy steel carts over and over again. Lunch was a potato and some thin soup, and dinner was turnip soup with a piece of black bread. Prisoners were often sick, but they were not treated for their illnesses. Those who were very ill were sent to the gas chamber to be put to death. Corrie watched as her sister became more and more sick. Eventually, Betsie died at the camp.

About one week later, Corrie was told to report after roll call. She wondered if she was going to be beaten again or, worse yet, shot. Instead, she was set free! She was given new clothes and a railway pass back to Holland. Soon after she left the camp, all women her age in the prison were killed. Later, Corrie learned she had been released by mistake. However, she knew God had saved her.

After her release, Corrie continued to tell others the good news about God, and she wrote several books about her experiences.

Brain Builders

 What were some things Corrie did that were courageous? What heroic characteristics did Corrie possess? Sketch a picture showing one heroic characteristic and share it with a friend. Ask your friend to guess which heroic characteristic you illustrated.

Why do you think Corrie helped the Jews? Would you risk your life to save someone? Why or why not?

Brain Builders

 Why do you think God allowed Corrie to be taken to the concentration camp? Research what life was like in concentration camps.

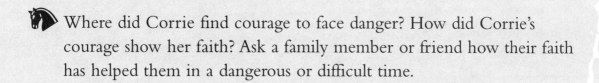 Where did Corrie find courage to face danger? How did Corrie's courage show her faith? Ask a family member or friend how their faith has helped them in a dangerous or difficult time.

Scout It Out!

 Read Joshua 2. Tell in what ways Rahab was courageous. Tell of someone who has been courageous like Rahab.

_____

_____

 Read 1 Samuel 17. Tell in what ways David was courageous. When might you need to be courageous like David?

_____

_____

_____

Scout It Out!

Read Daniel 3. Tell in what ways Shadrach, Meshach, and Abednego were courageous. Tell of someone who has been courageous like Shadrach, Meshach, and Abednego.

_____

_____

Read Daniel 6. Tell in what ways Daniel was courageous. When might you need to be courageous like Daniel?

_____

_____

_____

15

Bible Hero

Esther was a beautiful Jewish woman living as a captive in Babylon. She became the queen of Babylon through strange circumstances. God put her in a position to help his people in a time of need. Read her story in the Book of Esther. Write a page that Esther might have written in her journal.

Bible Hero

Write a journal page telling about a time you were courageous.

Equip Yourself

 Look through your local newspaper. Find a story about someone who showed courage. How was this person courageous?

_____

 We need courage for more than just dangerous situations. We need it for little things too. Listed below are several ways you can show your faith by modeling courage. Choose one way from the list below. Then on the next page sketch out a plan on how you will use the idea you chose to be courageous. If you like, add your own idea in the space provided.

Say no to someone who wants you to do something wrong.

Invite a new neighbor or friend to church.

Tell a friend about Jesus.

Stand up for someone who is being bullied.

Give up a bad habit.

Add your own:

_____

The Music Man
The Story of Keith Green

"If anyone speaks, he should do it as one speaking the very words of God. If anyone serves, he should do it with the strength God provides"

(1 Peter 4:11).

"The only music minister to whom the Lord will say, 'Well done, thou good and faithful servant,' is the one whose life proves what their lyrics are saying. Glorifying the only worthy One has to be a minister's most important goal."

—Keith Green

Keith Green first ran away from home when he was fifteen. He had a dream that overshadowed everything he did. He longed to be a brilliant music star.

Keith chased after fame and fortune, and his life spun out of control. He used drugs, experimented with mystical religions, and did other uncool things. Nothing made him happy.

When he was nineteen, Keith met and married Melody, a musician like him. Keith loved her very much, but he couldn't shake the feeling that something was missing. Then, when he was twenty-one, Keith found what he was looking for—Jesus Christ. After that, his life was never the same. He was forever changed.

Keith stopped his quest for stardom. Instead, he sang and wrote songs for the Lord. He sang about his love for God and how his life had been changed in awesome ways. When Keith took the stage, he would call out to his audience to strive to love God and put their faith into action: "If you praise and worship Jesus with your mouth and your life does not praise and worship him also, there's something wrong!"

Keith also quit drinking and doing drugs. He didn't need to do drugs to be cool anymore. He knew that God was what really mattered. He and Melody invited people into their home who wanted to kick their drug habit or get off the street. Keith and Melody were "Jesus with skin on" to the people around them. All of their work grew into "Last Day Ministries," which had over seventy new believers.

Because Keith kicked his drug habit and loved God so much, you would think his life would have been perfect. It wasn't. He still struggled with the same everyday problems everyone faces.

You would think his life would have been perfect, it wasn't. He still struggled.

So what did he do? He prayed constantly. He asked God to show him the sin in his life. He turned to his music. He wrote many songs during times when he struggled. Because Keith loved God so much, Keith wanted to please God in all he said and did. He even gave away some of his music to people for whatever they could afford.

People around the world heard God's message through Keith's music.

In the beginning, he played to small groups of about 20 people. Then God did something great. He blessed Keith's ministry. Over seven years the audience grew and grew and grew. Sometimes crowds of over 12,000 people listened to Keith's music!

Keith had many other great ideas of how he could glorify God. But that was not God's plan. On July 28, 1982, the small airplane Keith flew in crashed. It killed him and two of his children.

Because Keith was wholeheartedly devoted to using his talents to glorify God, people are still hearing the message of God's love. Keith's songs have been translated into many different languages and are still being heard around the world, long after his tragic death.

do it with the strength God provides

Brain Builders

 How did Keith Green use his talents to glorify God?

 Make a list of some ways Keith showed his faith through his actions.

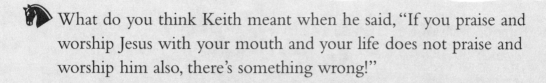

Brain Builders

What do you think Keith meant when he said, "If you praise and worship Jesus with your mouth and your life does not praise and worship him also, there's something wrong!"

What inspired some of Keith's best songs?

Think of a time you struggled. Write some lyrics or a poem that talks about your struggle and glorifies God.

Scout It Out!

 Read the parable of the talents in Matthew 25:14–30. What is the lesson in this parable? How does the parable apply to the skills and talents God gave you?

_____

_____

 Read Exodus 35:30–36:1. In this passage, the Israelites are preparing to build the tent of meeting where they will worship the Lord. Design a tent to worship the Lord.

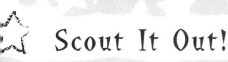

Scout It Out!

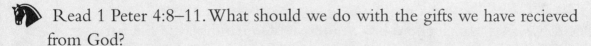

Read 1 Peter 4:8–11. What should we do with the gifts we have recieved from God?

_____

_____

Read 1 Samuel 3 and 1 Samuel 7. Tell about Samuel's gifts and his commitment to God. How can you be like Samuel?

_____

_____

_____

Bible Hero

David was a young shepherd boy who loved God and played the harp very well. God intended David to be the next king of Israel. King Saul had fallen out of God's favor, and God had allowed an evil spirit to torment Saul. Read 1 Samuel 16:14–23 to learn how David used his talent. Write a conversation that might have taken place between David and Saul.

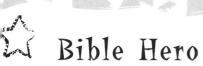

Bible Hero

Tell about a time you used a gift God gave you to help someone.

29

Equip Yourself

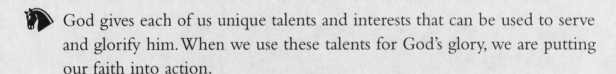 God gives each of us unique talents and interests that can be used to serve and glorify him. When we use these talents for God's glory, we are putting our faith into action.

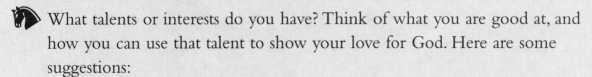 What talents or interests do you have? Think of what you are good at, and how you can use that talent to show your love for God. Here are some suggestions:

- Read a story or the Bible to someone younger. You could also read to an older person in a nursing home.
- Bake cookies to give to someone who is not feeling well or to welcome someone new in the neighborhood.
- Sing in the church choir.
- Write a letter to someone in the military.
- Rake leaves, mow the lawn, or shovel the sidewalk for someone who can't do it himself.
- Tell a joke to cheer someone up.
- Teach a younger brother or sister a new game.
- Collect food for a food drive.
- Run or walk to raise money for a good cause.
- Draw someone a picture.

Equip Yourself

List your talents and tell how you could use them this week.

An Incredible Adventure
The Story of Joni Eareckson Tada

Heroic Qualities: suffering, trust in God

"My flesh and my heart may fail,
but God is the strength of my heart
and my portion forever"
(Psalm 73:26).

"You know, you don't have to get a broken neck to be drawn to God. The truth is, people don't always listen to the experiences of others and learn from them. I hope you'll learn from my experience, though, and not have to go through the bitter lessons of suffering which I had to go through."

—Joni Eareckson Tada

Joni Eareckson was a girl who seemed to have everything going for her. A champion horse rider, she and her whole family loved athletics. They enjoyed playing tennis, hiking, and swimming together. Joni participated in soccer and other sports and was also a talented artist. Even though everything seemed to be on the right track for Joni, she needed to work on her character. Joni remembers that she was "headstrong and immature" as a teenager.

Joni Eareckson seemed to have everything.

"When I was in high school, I reacted to life selfishly and never built on any long-lasting values, and almost always at the expense of others," Joni explained.

Then, Joni heard about a Christian group called Young Life and decided to go to their camp.

While there, she heard the awesome message that Jesus died for her sins. She asked Jesus to come into her heart.

She accepted him as her Savior and asked God to change her life. "Lord, if you're really there, do something in my life to change me around," Joni prayed.

Not long after, on a July summer day, the unthinkable happened. Joni was in a terrible diving accident. She was just 18. Her neck was broken, and she was left paralyzed. There would be no more horseback riding, tennis, hiking, swimming, or soccer. And, without the use of her hands, there would be no more art—or so it seemed. Later, Joni thought back, "July 30, 1967 was the beginning of an incredible adventure."

Then the unthinkable happened.

Joni spent two difficult years in rehabilitation and physical therapy. She could do nothing for herself. She couldn't feed or bathe herself. She couldn't dress herself or even brush her own hair! Her faith in God was severely tested. Joni often felt very sorry for herself and became depressed.

One good thing happened during this tough time. Joni's friends read to her from the Bible. She was comforted when they read God's Word. But, when they read from other philosophers, the words seemed emptier. The Bible was the key. It satisfied and comforted her. Joni made a decision to rely on God's Word and claim his promises of love and protection. She trusted that God would take care of her.

Joni thought her art days were gone forever. But God in his eternal wisdom and grace had other plans for Joni. One day, a therapist urged Joni to draw with her mouth. Joni spent months and months learning how to draw and paint with a brush clenched between her teeth. She began creating outstanding artwork! A man saw her work and organized a special exhibit for her. It was a sold-out event. Then, newspaper reporters began to write about Joni, and she received invitations to speak at churches.

Joni also did a television appearance. She spoke to millions of people about her new life of suffering. This appearance helped start a new ministry, "Joni and Friends." Joni began speaking to and helping those with disabilities. Her ministry is still going strong today.

Joni's diving accident changed the direction of her life. Since then, she has written over 30 books. All of them glorify God! She has also created many finely detailed paintings. They are in high demand. God has blessed her work.

Joni still does not have the use of her arms and legs. But through God's grace she is at peace: "Only God knows why I was paralyzed. Maybe he knew I'd be ultimately happier serving him…. I wouldn't change my life for anything…. I'm really thankful he did something to get my attention and change me."

Brain Builders

 Create a list of the events of Joni's life in order.

 How did Joni show trust in God? Talk to a friend or parent about how they show trust in God.

36

Brain Builders

What do you think about Joni's statement, "I wouldn't change my life for anything.... I'm really thankful he did something to get my attention and change me"?

Joni has a ministry helping the disabled and speaking to them and others about God. Explain the value of this ministry.

Scout It Out!

 Read Romans 5:3–5. List the qualities that suffering produces.

_____

_____

_____

 Read 1 Peter 4:19. What does this verse tell us about suffering?

_____

_____

_____

Scout It Out!

Read Romans 8:28. How does this verse make you feel?

_____

_____

_____

Read Isaiah 55:8–9. How do these verses apply to suffering?

_____

_____

_____

Bible Hero

Job was a man who loved God. He had everything anyone would want—wealth, land, and a large, loving family. Satan told God that if those things were taken away from Job, then Job would curse God. God allowed Job to be tested through suffering. Read Job 1, 2, 3, and 42. Use the Venn diagram to compare Joni and Job.

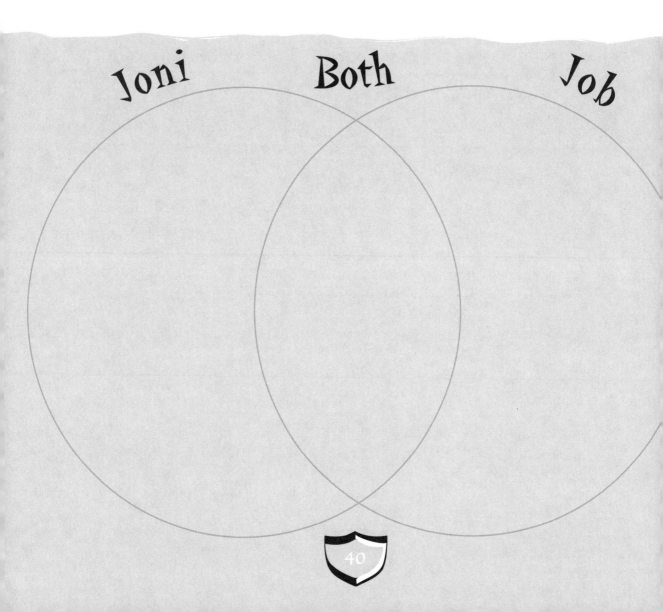

Joni   Both   Job

Bible Hero

Now compare yourself with Joni in the Venn Diagram below.

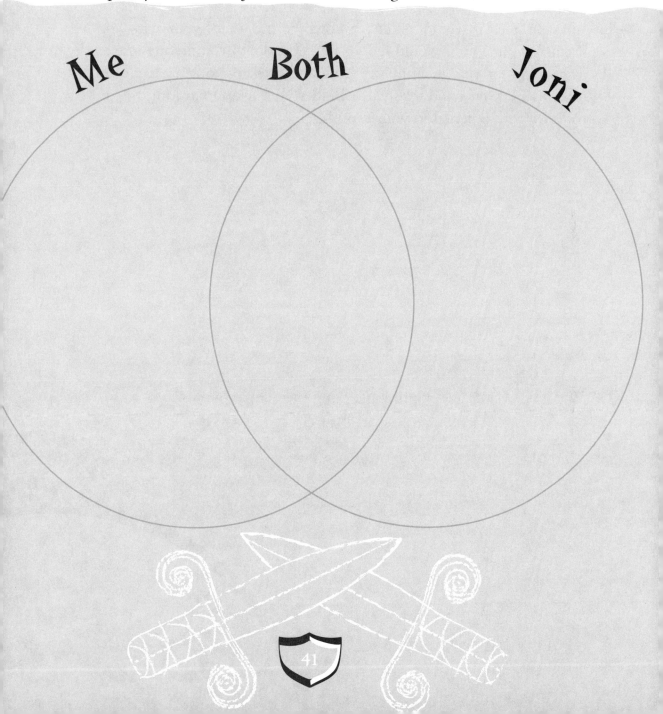

Me

Both

Joni

41

Equip Yourself

 Imagine what it would be like to not have the use of your arms and legs. Think about how it would feel to be dependent on someone else to do everything for you, including feeding and dressing you. Try to do some things with your hands clasped behind your back. Do as Joni did and try to draw with a pencil in your mouth.

 Write what you were thinking during the activity above.

Equip Yourself

Make a plan to help someone who is suffering.

Talk with your family about your ideas. Some things you can do:

- Visit children in the hospital and read to or play a game with them.
- Cook a meal for a needy family.
- Do a chore for someone who is physically not able.
- Give a hug to someone who is grieving.
- Be friendly when you see someone in a wheelchair.

Looking in the Face of Death
The Story of Al Braca

Heroic Qualities: service to God, dedication to his mission

"But the Lord stood at my side and gave me strength, so that through me the message might be fully proclaimed and all the Gentiles might hear it. And I was delivered from the lion's mouth. The Lord will rescue me from every evil attack and will bring me safely to his heavenly kingdom"

(2 Timothy 4:17–18).

"I knew he would stop to help and minister to people but I never thought for a minute that he wouldn't come home."
—Jeannie Braca, wife of Al Braca

Al Braca's heart was breaking. "God, please help her," he prayed.

Al and Jeannie Braca's four-year-old daughter had a rare blood disease. Chances were that she would die. Even though the Bracas didn't know God, they went to him for help—and God answered. Al and Jeannie's young daughter was miraculously healed!

Al also touched the lives of people in his workplace. Al worked in Tower One of the World Trade Center in New York City. Many of the people there desperately needed God. Although Al would have liked to work somewhere else, he felt God wanted him to stay and talk to his coworkers about God—to be a light in the darkness. Many of them sarcastically

Al had not been at work long when a terrorist crashed an airplane into the World Trade Center.

After that, Al and Jeannie shared the love of God with everyone. They found a church and served in many ways. A friend of Al's said, "He was a bigger-than-life kind of person. He was full of joy and fun to be with…. He loved the Lord with all of his heart and mind and soul. He lived to serve the Lord and to serve other people."

According to Jeannie, Al always said his ministry began at home, and he lived what he preached. When Jeannie was sick for two years, Al took care of her and the children.

called him "The Rev" (short for Reverend). That didn't stop Al Braca. He continued to pray that the people he worked with would come to know God.

On September 11, 2001, Al Braca faced the ultimate test of his faith. On that morning, Al had not been at work long when a terrorist crashed an airplane into the World Trade Center. Jeannie looked on helplessly as she watched the crash on television. Her faith was also being tested.

"I knew he would stop to help and minister to people, but I never thought for a minute that he wouldn't come home," she said. But Al never made it home. The World Trade Center Towers collapsed and hundreds of people died, including Al Braca.

Al realized they were trapped in the building and were not going to escape.

After the attack, reports started to come out about those last minutes of life on the 105th floor—the floor Al worked on, which was above the floor where the plane crashed. Many of the people Al worked with called home or sent e-mails at the last minute to their families. Many told that a man named

Al was leading them in prayer. It appears that when Al realized they were trapped in the building and were not going to escape, instead of panicking he continued to carry out his mission. Al led a group of fifty people in prayer and shared with them how Jesus Christ died for their sins. We don't know how many of those people may have come to know Jesus Christ in those final minutes of their lives because of Al's witness.

Though Jeannie did not get to talk to Al that day before the Towers collapsed, she learned that, in the middle of it all, Al had tried to reach his family. A month after the tragedy, an MCI operator contacted Jeannie and told her that Al had tried to call but was unable to get through. He had asked the operator to contact his family: "Tell them, I love them."

Brain Builders

 Write a note to Al telling what you think about his service.

 Make a list of Al's heroic qualities.

Brain Builders

Why did Al stay with his job? Can you relate to his feeling? Explain.

How do you think God felt about Al's last act of service?

Scout It Out!

Read the Great Commission in Matthew 28:16–20. In what ways are we to serve God? How have you fulfilled the Great Commission?

_____

_____

Read the Book of Jonah. Tell a friend about Jonah's service to God.

_____

_____

_____

_____

Scout It Out!

Read 2 Corinthians 9:6–15. What did Paul say about service? How does Al Braca's life display the service Paul talked about?

_____

_____

_____

Read Romans 10:13–15. List the four steps that lead someone to be saved.

_____

_____

_____

_____

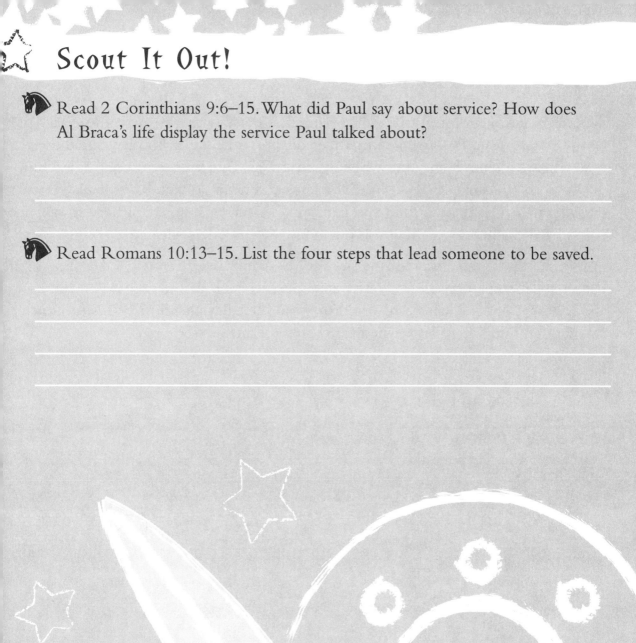

Bible Hero

The apostle Paul (originally called Saul) was possibly the greatest missionary of all time. Paul was a Pharisee and member of the Sanhedrin who persecuted the new Christian church and threw believers into jail. But after Jesus confronted him on the road to Damascus, Paul lived for Jesus and never looked back. Paul was stoned, shipwrecked, jailed, and was later put to death. Paul did not have to die; he could have claimed his right as a Roman citizen and been released.

Read parts of the amazing story of Paul in Acts 8:1–3; 9:1–31; 14:8–20; 16:16–40; and chapters 25–28. Write an e-mail to Paul. Include what you think about his actions and why you would or would not have liked to be his missionary partner. Tell him what you learned from him and his service.

To: Paul-the-Missionary@heaven.com

Re: Your Witness

Bible Hero

Write a letter that Paul might have written to Al Braca or to people involved in the World Trade Center tragedy.

53

Equip Yourself

 It is sometimes scary to share the gospel. However, sharing the gospel of Jesus Christ is not always done with words; it is also shared through actions, such as those of Al Braca when he cared for his wife and family. The gospel is shared each time you put your faith into action.

Think of the people around you: your family, friends, and neighbors. What are some ways you can share the gospel with them? How can you serve God through others?

Equip Yourself

Talk with your parents and/or church leaders about taking a group to serve in a homeless shelter, soup kitchen, or other inner-city ministry. Give up a Saturday or a holiday to make sure the needy see and hear the gospel of Jesus Christ. Tell about your experience.

An Olympic Faith
The Story of Jackie Joyner-Kersey

Heroic Qualities: spiritual strength, endurance

"I have told you these things so that in me
you may have peace. In this world you will
have trouble. But take heart!
I have overcome the world"

(John 16:33).

"Mom would always tell me, 'Jackie, no matter what, always strive to be a good person.' From her I learned that whatever you do is a test of character, a test of heart. Will you choose a godly path, or your own? That was crucial for me—especially living in the inner city."

—Jackie Joyner-Kersey

Jackie, a little girl growing up in the inner city of East St. Louis, loved to run. But more than anything, she wanted to be the world's best track athlete. When she was nine, she entered her first race, a 400-meter run. She finished in last place. "That taught me I didn't have to win," explained Jackie. "I could learn just as much or more from not winning, such as how to do it better next time."

Jackie saw someone killed in front of her home when she was eleven years old, and her grandmother was shot and killed when Jackie was only twelve.

Growing up in the inner city of East St. Louis, Jackie experienced some things that were traumatic and would be tough for anyone to handle.

Jackie saw someone killed in front of her home when she was eleven years old, and her grandmother was shot and killed when Jackie was only twelve.

Her mother died from meningitis when Jackie was nineteen, and later that year Jackie learned she had asthma. Many people would have struggled coping with all of the pain and anguish, but Jackie leaned on her family and God through it all.

Because Jackie's parents were Christians, Jackie accepted Jesus as her Savior when she was quite young. They went to church every Sunday. She credits her parents with helping to keep her on track with school, sports, and God: "My parents assured us that we could be 'somebody.' And that everyone had a purpose in life—it was just a question of finding it and living it. It was their strength and determination that kept me away from drugs and alcohol."

Today you would never know that Jackie Joyner-Kersey lost that first race. She has won three Olympic gold medals, one silver, two bronze, and four World Championship gold medals. She also holds the Olympic and world records in the heptathlon, the American long jump, and the 50- and 60-meter hurdles. Jackie has amazing strength and endurance as an athlete. Even more important, as a Christian, Jackie has amazing spiritual strength and endurance.

Jackie now tries to give something back to her hometown so youth know they can change their lives as well. She's funded a youth center in East St. Louis, donated a scholarship to a National Merit Scholar from her old high school, had teams of children from her old neighborhood participate in Junior Olympics, and much more.

To Jackie, her faith and the race she is running here on earth are the most important things in her life. "God is the one who gave me success, and he can take it away if I don't handle it well. Knowing where my true worth and success comes from puts it in the right perspective." Jackie says that God has been with her all the way and she knows that is where her true strength comes from. One of her favorite verses is Philippians 4:13: "I can do all things through him who strengthens me."

Jackie would love all kids to overcome their challenges and find their dreams. When she was nine years old and lost that race, who would have thought she would one day be an all-star athlete? For Jackie, Matthew 17:20 says it all. "I tell you the truth, if you have faith as small as a mustard seed, you can say to this mountain, 'Move from here to there,' and it will move. Nothing will be impossible for you."

I have overcome the world.

Brain Builders

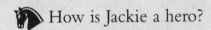 How is Jackie a hero?

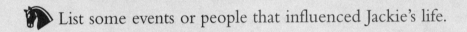 List some events or people that influenced Jackie's life.

Brain Builders

 What would Jackie say about winning?

How does Jackie's life compare with your own?

Scout It Out!

 Read Philippians 4:13. Why do you think this was one of Jackie's favorite verses?

_____

_____

_____

 Read Luke 22:39–45. Tell about Jesus' spiritual strength and endurance the night before his crucifixion.

_____

_____

_____

Scout It Out!

 Read 1 Corinthians 9:24–27. Design a brochure that advertises running the race of life like Paul talks about. Think about these questions.

How does Paul say we should run the race of life?

What kind of training do you think would help us in our race?

What does it mean to run for a crown that will last?

Bible Hero

Samson was a man born with great strength. However, Samson did not always use his strength wisely. He often used it to bring himself glory, though he did redeem himself in the end. Read the story of Samson in Judges 13–16. Write a list of interview questions you would like to ask Samson about his physical and spiritual strength.

Bible Hero

Answer your interview questions as if you were Samson.

Equip Yourself

Jackie Joyner-Kersey has great physical strength but even greater spiritual strength. Part of her spiritual strength comes from the fact that she takes time to be with God, to pray, and to read his Word.

Do you have problems in your life? Bring them to the Lord in prayer. Write your prayer below.

Equip Yourself

Make a plan, by yourself or as a family, to spend time every day praying and reading the Bible. Start with only five minutes each day and add a minute or two every few days until you are spending twenty to thirty minutes or more in prayer and Bible reading. If you would like to build up your physical strength as well, take a walk and pray while you walk.

One Smooth Stone
The Story of David and Goliath

Heroic Qualities: faith, bravery, determination, loyalty

"Have I not commanded you? Be strong and courageous. Do not be terrified; do not be discouraged, for the LORD your God will be with you wherever you go"

(Joshua 1:9).

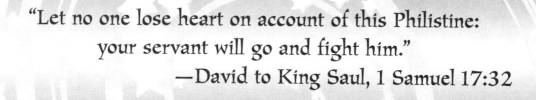

"Let no one lose heart on account of this Philistine:
your servant will go and fight him."
—David to King Saul, 1 Samuel 17:32

"Choose a man and have him come down to me!" shouted the giant. "If he kills me, we will become your subjects. If I kill him, you will become our subjects and serve us. Give me a man and let us fight each other!"

King Saul and the Israelite army shook with fear. They were at war with the Philistines, an ungodly nation. The Philistines were located on one hill and the Israelites on another. Between them lay a valley.

Every day, the Philistines sent out their champion to taunt Israel. His name was Goliath, and he was over nine feet tall! Each day for forty days, he came out and demanded that they send out a man to fight him.

His name was Goliath, and he was over nine feet tall!

David was a young shepherd boy whose brothers fought with King Saul in the Israelite army. One morning, David's father, Jesse, gave David some food to take to his brothers. Jesse also wanted David to find out how his brothers were doing. David went to the Israelite camp with the supplies and greeted his brothers just as the armies were drawing up their battle lines.

As he watched, Goliath came out and taunted the Israelite army. They all ran.

David looked on in disbelief. "What will be done for the man who kills this Philistine?" David asked the men near him. "Who is this Philistine that he should defy the armies of the living God?"

The men told David that the king would give great wealth to the man who killed Goliath, as well as the king's daughter in marriage. Moreover, the man's family would never have to pay taxes again.

When the king learned of David's questions, Saul had David brought before him. "Why do you ask about this?" asked Saul.

"Let no one lose heart because of this Philistine. Your servant will fight him," announced David.

"You will not be able to fight him," said Saul. "You are only a boy, and this Philistine has been a fighting man from his youth."

David then told Saul that while he watched his father's sheep, he had killed many wild animals, including lions and bears.

"The Lord who delivered me from the paws of the lion and the bear will deliver me from the hand of the Philistine," he said.

Saul dressed David in his armor. David could not walk in the armor, so he took it off. He decided to fight Goliath just as he was. David chose five smooth stones from the stream and put them in the pouch in his shepherd's bag. Then he set off to face the Philistine with his staff and sling in his hand.

> "The Lord who delivered me from the paws of the lion and the bear will deliver me from the hand of the Philistine," he said.

Goliath laughed when he saw David was only a boy.

"What am I, a dog, that you come after me with a stick?" he rumbled. "Come here and let me feed your flesh to the birds!"

As Goliath moved closer, David ran forward to meet him. David reached into his bag, pulled out one smooth stone, and put it in his sling. Then he slung the stone at Goliath and hit him in the forehead. The mighty giant tumbled to the ground.

"Come here and let me feed your flesh to the birds."

"You come against me with sword and spear and javelin, but I come against you in the name of the Lord Almighty," challenged David. "He is the Lord of the army of Israel and you have defied him. This day he will hand you over to me, and I will strike you down dead and the whole world will know that there is a God in Israel, for the battle is the Lord's."

David ran and pulled out Goliath's sword and killed Goliath with it. When the Philistines saw Goliath was dead, they turned and ran, with the Israelites shouting and running behind them in hot pursuit.

From that day on, Saul kept David in his service, and David did not return to tend sheep for his father.

the LORD your God will be with you wherever you go

73

Brain Builders

 Jot down what David said to Goliath in your own words.

 Make a list of how David was faithful.

74

Brain Builders

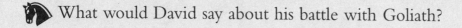 Circle the words that you think best describe Goliath.

kind   faithful   loving

smart   muscular   arrogant

fast   jolly   huge

powerful   proud   saintly

 What would David say about his battle with Goliath?

Scout It Out!

 Read Hebrews 11. Write a note to a biblical person telling why you admire his or her faith.

_____

_____

 Read about the faith of the centurion in Matthew 8:5–10. When might you need to be faithful like the centurion?

_____

_____

_____

Scout It Out!

 Read Matthew 8:23–27. What advice would the disciples give you about faith?

_____

_____

Read Matthew 17:14–20. Draw a picture to illustrate these verses.

77

Bible Hero

After Moses' death, God used Joshua to lead the Israelites into the Promised Land. Before the Israelites could take over the land, they had to get the ungodly people out. The first battle the Israelites fought was the battle of Jericho. Joshua needed great faith to fight this battle because the Lord chose an odd way for them to win. Read Joshua 5:13–6:27. Design a video game of Joshua fighting the battle of Jericho. Include obstacles that Joshua must overcome. Remember, Joshua's power and success came from his faith. Be sure to incorporate this into your game.

Bible Hero

Write about the characters in your video game here.

Equip Yourself

 Many of the men and women of our country have fought bravely and served our country with loyalty because they have faith in our "one nation under God." Here are some things you can do to recognize them.

Send a card or letter to a veteran telling him or her how much you appreciate what he has done.

Tie a yellow ribbon around a tree in your yard for those still serving overseas.

Interview a veteran for a school project.

Ask a veteran about his experiences and ask if you can see his medals.

Equip Yourself

Think about your faith. Are you calm during the storms of life, or are you frightened as the disciples were? Prayer and memorizing Scripture are two of the best defenses against fear. They help to make your faith in God strong. Memorize Joshua 1:9 and Philippians 4:13 and pray that God will help you to remember them the next time a storm comes your way. Write out your prayer. Remember, the battle belongs to the Lord!

A Mother's Love
The Story of Mother Teresa

Heroic Qualities: selflessness, love

"Dear children, let us not love with words
or tongue but with actions and in truth"

(1 John 3:18).

"We too must give to each other until it hurts. It is not enough for us to say: 'I love God, but I do not love my neighbor.' Saint John says that you are a liar if you say you love God and you don't love your neighbor."

—Mother Teresa

Mother Teresa was riding a train to Darjeeling in India when she felt God's call—he was calling her to serve him among the poorest of the poor in India. She had been serving God for many years, but this was to be a turning point in her life.

Gonxhe Bojaxhiu, Mother Teresa, was born in Albania in 1910. Her parents were devoted Catholics and always prayed and went to church. They taught their daughter well. Their care for the poor and needy left a lasting impact on their young daughter's life.

By the time she was twelve years old, she knew she wanted to be a nun. When she was nineteen years old, she joined a convent and lived in India for twenty years, where she became the principal for the Catholic High School.

She heard God's call and decided to minister to those who had no one to love them.

84

It was at this point, when Mother Teresa was thirty-eight years old, that she heard God's call and decided to minister to those who had no one to love them and care for them. She went into one of the poorest places in the world—the slums of Calcutta. It was there that she began the Missionaries of Charity.

The Missionaries of Charity ministered to the sick and hungry. Mother Teresa gave love, food, and clothing to all who came to her doors.

She said her mission was "to care for the hungry, the naked, the homeless, the crippled, the blind, the lepers, all those people who feel unwanted, unloved, uncared for throughout society, people that have become a burden to the society and are shunned by everyone."

Mother Teresa gave love, food, and clothing to all who came to her doors.

Mother Teresa's work did not stop there. She hated to see the poorest people dying in the streets and wanted a place for them. With the help and permission of officials in Calcutta, she converted part of an abandoned Hindu temple into a home for the dying. It was a place where even the poorest could go.

Soon after, she had another home built for the dying, followed by a leper colony, and then an orphanage for the orphaned children of India.

What was it that drove Mother Teresa to show this kind of love and selflessness for her fellow human beings? It was Jesus! "He died for you and for me, and for that leper, and for that man dying of hunger, and that naked person lying in the street—not only of Calcutta, but of Africa, and New York, and London, and Oslo—and insisted that we love one another as he loves each one of us," professed Mother Teresa.

She said her mission was "to care for the hungry, the naked, the homeless, the crippled, the blind, the lepers, all those people who feel unwanted, unloved, uncared for throughout society, people that have become a burden to the society and are shunned by everyone."

Mother Teresa became a well-known champion of the poor and gave many speeches around the world. She also received many awards, including the 1979 Nobel Peace Prize. When she learned the Nobel committee was giving a dinner to recognize her, she asked the committee to cancel it and instead use the money to feed four hundred hungry children in India for a year.

Mother Teresa did not feel that everyone should rush out into the street to care for the poor. Instead, she said our love should begin at home.

"Just get together, love one another, bring that peace, that joy, that strength of presence of each other into the home.... Love begins at home, and it is not how much we do, but how much love we put in the action that we do."

Mother Teresa's work has grown into 570 missions around the world, with over 100,000 nuns and volunteers running homes for AIDS, leprosy, and tuberculosis patients; soup kitchens; children's and family counseling programs; orphanages; and schools.

Mother Teresa died in 1997 at the age of eighty-seven.

Brain Builders

 Circle the words that describe Mother Teresa.

angry   silly   spiritual
selfless   arrogant   fake
loving   humble   proud

 Draw a picture of where Mother Teresa said we should begin showing
God's love.

Brain Builders

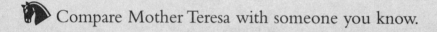

Compare Mother Teresa with someone you know.

Write a thank-you note to Mother Teresa.

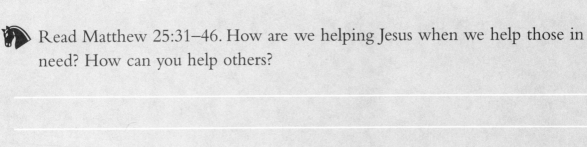

Scout It Out!

Read Matthew 25:31–46. How are we helping Jesus when we help those in need? How can you help others?

_____

_____

_____

Read John 13:34–35. How are we to love one another? What does this verse mean to you in your life?

_____

_____

_____

☆ Scout It Out!

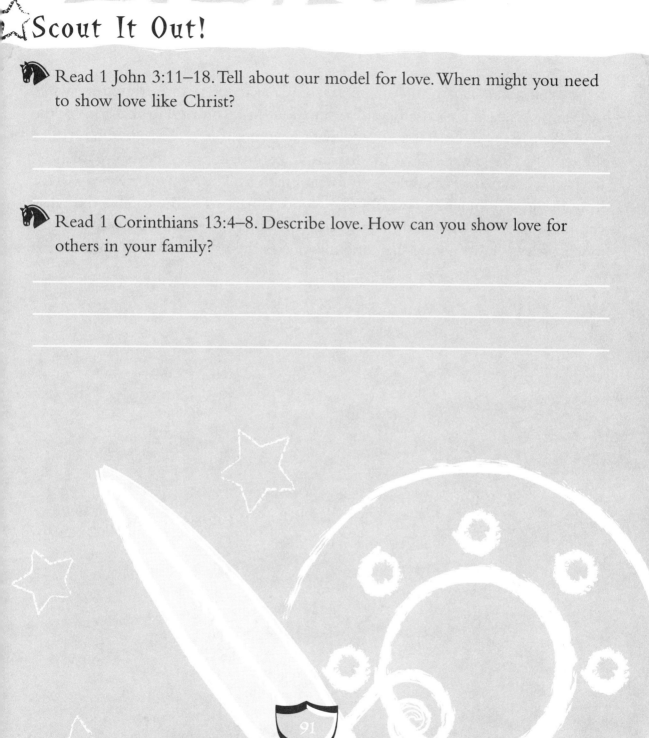

🐴 Read 1 John 3:11–18. Tell about our model for love. When might you need to show love like Christ?

_____

_____

_____

🐴 Read 1 Corinthians 13:4–8. Describe love. How can you show love for others in your family?

_____

_____

_____

Bible Hero

Jesus often told parables to teach great truths. A parable is an earthly story with a heavenly meaning. Jesus used familiar situations in his stories. In the story of the Good Samaritan, the priest and the Levite were both men of God who served at the temple. The Jews despised the Samaritan people, because they were formerly Jews who had married people from foreign nations. The Samaritans stayed away from the Jews as much as possible. The Good Samaritan in the parable did what was unpopular but right and loving. Read the parable in Luke 10:25–37. Write a modern-day parable giving the same message as the parable of the Good Samaritan.

Bible Hero

Write a story or poem about your favorite hero. What heroic qualities does this person display? Be creative.

Equip Yourself

Think about those in your family who might be hurting or need your help. What can you do to ease their pain? Here are some suggestions—and smile when you do them. Remember that you are doing these things for Jesus!

- Do dishes or other household chores.
- Help a brother or sister with homework.
- Help cook dinner.
- Give your mom or sister a sincere compliment.
- Tell your brother how good he is at something.
- Give someone a present without a reason.
- Go to your brother or sister's game and cheer for them.
- Make up your own list of things that you can do every day.

Equip Yourself

A way to show God's love to the poor and needy is to volunteer at a homeless shelter or other mission. Talk with your parents about volunteering there as a family project. Another way to show love to the poor and needy is to sponsor a child from another country. When you do this, you send money every month to help feed and clothe the child. You will get a picture and letters from the child, and you can write back as well. It is a great feeling to know that you are helping a child who would otherwise go hungry.